Believing is Seeing

Daily Journal of Transformation

by maya gonzalez

31 day workbook

❋ For Zai, Sky, & Matthew ❋

Copyright © 2015 by Maya Christina Gonzalez.
Published by Reflection Press, San Francisco, California.
All rights reserved. Printed in the USA
ISBN 978-0-9843799-9-6
Library of Congress Control Number: 2015956963
Book Design by Matthew SG

"create a new reality" ~ www.reflectionpress.com
Reflection Press is an independent publisher of radical children's books and works that expand spiritual and cultural awareness.

Believing is Seeing Online Course
This workbook grew out of the online course, *Believing is Seeing: Daily Journal of Transformation* taught through School of the Free Mind. The 31 day course uses the *I See Peace* book as a framework and guide coupled with the *Daily Peace* pocket reader and this *Believing is Seeing* workbook to transform everyday habits and open up to peace.

More about the course: www.schoolofthefreemind.com/peace

Welcome, Welcome!

I'm so very happy that you're here. Any and all steps you take toward peace are highly valuable and matter more than you may ever know. I know that your steps affect me and the world I live in. So always I am grateful for each one.

This work has the potential to be as deep and transformative as you wish it to be. I encourage you to go slow and steady. You have the potential to learn great things about yourself, about the world we live in and how we can create lasting and far reaching change. I already have immense faith in you. I know the power that lies within you. Take a moment to pause and sense that power, all that potential already expressed and all that lies latent within your deepest self. What you do here matters. You change the world as you change yourself.

The journey through this book is similar to my own healing journey. Ultimately, it is about self awareness and building a strong foundation of skills to creatively express your life freely and powerfully. Using peace as a learning point provides the perfect frame to play with your personal beliefs while supporting yourself and our world.

What's more, there is no end to how deep or how expanded peace can reach. There is no end to peace! As you commit to 31 days of exploring peace in your life now, know that you are setting the stage for future journeys. You will find the power of gentle repetition naturally supports you in finding your own style of transformation. Peace is a lifetime. You can return to this journey again and again and learn something fresh and meaningful about yourself and the world each time.

The journey begins. You are peace. Peace is now.

love,
maya

create a new reality
reflection press
unCommon fruit series

PREPARING FOR THE JOURNEY

GATHERING ADDITIONAL MATERIALS

All you really need to start your 31 day journey is a pencil or pen, BUT if you'd like to gather some additional materials to compliment your journey, here are my suggestions:

☀ THE *I See Peace* BOOK/JOURNAL

This workbook uses the *i see peace* book (or e-book) as a framework for the materials presented for 31 days. The spread from the e-book is shown on each day for reference and allows the workbook to stand alone if you don't have the *i see peace* book.

i see peace was created with the idea that you could draw and write all over the pages. If you have the book, I encourage you to write your affirmations, what you're trying to create, your hopes and dreams, even the things you're trying to let go of directly on the pages of your *i see peace* book. It serves as a holding place for your larger lessons and thoughts.

☀ ART MATERIALS

Through the journey you will be invited to make art. The pages are made of 70# paper. That means you are free to experiment with a wide range of art materials. Allow yourself to be guided by what feels the most expressive and fluid. Your style, just like your materials may be very simple or complex or everywhere in between! Listen to your creative self.

Also, feel free to mix things up. Experiment. Play!
For example: Crayons and watercolors; color pencils and acrylic markers; ink and gouache; collage and watercolors

Drawing materials:
- Crayons
- Color Pencils
- Pencils
- Markers
- Acrylic Pens
- Ink Pens
- Pens
- Color Pens

More materials:
- Collage with glue stick: Personal photos, magazine clippings, pieces of art, drawings, journal entries, printed words, notes, cards, etc...

Materials that bleed through page:
- Permanent markers
- Ink and brush

Materials that smear:
*place sheet of parchment or wax paper between pages
- Hard or Soft pastels
- Oil pastels
- Charcoal

Materials that need to dry:
*clip book open until the art is dry to prevent pages from drying together
- Watercolors
- Acrylic paints
- Glitter glue!

SETTING TIME ASIDE EACH DAY

There are many different ways that you can journey through this workbook. No one way is better than another. You may find that you want to engage in **every single element** presented to you. Or you may find yourself intuitively **drawn to only play with one or two elements.** Trust that you will be **guided to participate in the way that is right for you.**

Consider setting aside a part of each day to focus on peace. It can be comforting to tie peace to a familiar ritual, like morning coffee or just before bed as you wind down from the day. Or both! Or you may integrate peace into your full day's routine, keeping it a constant focus on some level. Just making the commitment to peace opens the door. **Remember every step counts.**

ABOUT THE DAILY COMPONENTS

Through gentle, repetitive behaviors you become more aware of your thoughts and consequently your beliefs about your self, your world, what's possible, and more. You begin by playing with your beliefs about peace as a way to not only bring more peace into your life and the world, but also to learn how to transform beliefs that are not serving you.

Each day will have:

DAILY THOUGHTS

Short paragraphs that talk briefly about the lesson of the day. These will also relate to the spread of the day from the *i see peace* book. You'll be working through *i see peace* a spread a day starting on Day 2.

"A QUICK-BITE-OF-PEACE" AFFIRMATIONS

Supportive phrases that you are welcome to repeat throughout the day. If an affirmation feels particularly relevant feel free to take it on as your own for a while. You can play with it for as long as you like. Similarly, feel free to adjust the affirmations to accommodate what feels right for you to say. You want the words to feel personal or at the very least have an open, curious stance in relation to them.

There are two versions of the affirmations. The short sweet version (in bold) that you can repeat over and over like a prayer and the fuller version that you can sit with longer.

GUERILLA PEACE

Fun suggestions to play with bringing more peace into your life and the world around you.

JOURNAL PROMPTS

Brief writing prompts that provide the opportunity to go deeper into the daily lesson.

THOUGHT PROMPTS

Paying attention to your thoughts is one of the skills that you're developing. Thought prompts will bring greater awareness to different areas of thought.

ART PROMPTS

As you open up to more ways of knowing beyond the linear, rational style, words may not always serve you. Reclaiming nonverbal ways of knowing, expressing and communicating is very supportive. If you're accustomed to expressing yourself visually or if you would like to open up to a new skill, this is here.

EXTRA PEACE TREATS & EXTRA STRENGTH PEACE*

Spread throughout the journey (*on some days), are additional worksheets to take a deeper look at beliefs and emotions.

NOW LET'S BEGIN 31 DAYS OF PEACE...

DAY 1

TODAY'S SPREAD from *i see peace*

❋ Daily Thought

With the momentum of new beginnings and the power that rises from within, we begin *Believing is Seeing*. Just like the title of the book states, we will be working with our beliefs as we open ourselves up to see a new life, a new way of being, even create a new, more powerful habit of support for ourselves and the planet. Take a moment and review the last year. What aches and pains, what joys and triumphs, what lessons learned or unlearned? Notice everything. When you acknowledge and accept what is without judgment, you open doors to greater creative flow. This is the day to begin. **Peace begins now.**

❋ Affirmation

Peace begins now. With every breath I breathe in peace, with every breath I breathe out stress. For a moment I allow the entire last year to rest on my breath-- as I breathe in, I hold onto each moment of love deep in my being and as I breathe out, I let go of each worry, fear, hurt and anger and I breathe in again.
Peace begins now.

a quick BITe of peace

The Compliment of Beauty...
tell someone
"that looks beautiful on you"
or
"you look beautiful in that."

guerrilla peace

❋ Guerilla Peace

DAY 1

TODAY'S DATE: _____

❋ Journal Prompt

What compelled you to take this 31 day journey? What do you sincerely hope to get out of it? How do you hope this affects this next year for you?

❋ Thought Prompt

What are 3 random thoughts you noticed having today?

pg. 5

DAY 1

TODAY'S SPREAD
from *i see peace*

✹ Art Prompt

Show your relationship with peace on this drawing.

For example, is it close by, within you, far away, conceptual, complicated, desired, doubted, blooming...If you'd like you can symbolize peace with flowers like in the *i see peace* book.

DAY 1

TODAY'S DATE: _____

pg. 7

DAY 2

what is peace?

TODAY'S SPREAD from *i see peace*

❋ Daily Thought

Peace. What is peace? The question inside of this question is, do I feel peace? We cannot fully know something if we haven't had the experience ourselves. It is always best to begin where you are. Honestly look at your life, your heart, your private self and ask, *do I feel peace?*

You may be confused about whether you feel peace or not. It may seem that you feel peace in certain areas or certain times and not others. Determine if peace touches all of your life or if it is isolated to certain areas. If you find that you feel peace, pay close attention to what this feeling is. *How would you explain it to someone?*

If you feel like you don't really know what peace is personally and you don't think you feel peace in general, this is equally good to notice. **Bringing awareness immediately begins changing things.**

❋ Affirmation

When I bring awareness to my thoughts and beliefs they begin to transform. I begin to open up to the real power of my thoughts and beliefs. And even though I feel like I still have a lot to learn, I trust that this will make my learning more effective until it is effortless.

a quick BITE of peace

❋ Guerilla Peace

With one person you come into contact with in public...
make a point of asking how they're doing and be open to listening for a moment. Perhaps ask how their last year went and what their hopes are for the following year.

pg. 8

DAY 2

TODAY'S DATE:

❋ Journal Prompt

Do you believe real peace is possible? For you? For your community? For your country? For the world?

Thought Prompt

What are 3 things you do every morning? What thoughts do you tend to have during these 3 things?

DAY 2

what is peace?

TODAY'S SPREAD from *i see peace*

✻ Art Prompt

Draw or write what you would love to see in terms of peace in the four different areas on the *Fantasy World* worksheet.

Some ideas are to use bullet points to list your main thoughts to pack a lot of information in a small space, or use the worksheet as a place to begin and then take your drawing or writing further in your *i see peace* book. Use your biggest imagination to dream up your own fantasy peace life, your community's, your country's and your world's. Allow your thoughts of peace to expand to include these multiple levels of experience.

DAY 3

TODAY'S SPREAD from i see peace

> like many things in life peace is not what i thought it was.

✸ Daily Thought

Often we have *"pie in the sky"* notions of what peace is. Lofty, brightly lit illusions that give a sense of hope and possibility, but are not actually felt, experienced and relatable on a more mundane level. Seeing through the illusion of what we would like to think peace is begins to bring real peace more into reach. Open up to see if you have illusions about peace. Illusions that may have kept peace unattainable.

✸ Affirmation

I can see through any limited thinking as I open up to the possibility that deep and constant peace is available to me at all times. My natural state of being is peaceful, keeping me strong and flexible through all the amazing times in my life. My thinking is opening up now.

a quick BITe of peace

Be specifically generous to someone while you are driving or something similar...
For example pay for someone's toll, give someone the parking space you just found, trusting that you will find another.

guerrilla peace

✸ Guerilla Peace

DAY 3

TODAY'S DATE:

✻ Journal Prompt

Does peace attainable? What comes to mind when you imagine what may stand between you and your peace?

✻ Thought Prompt

What kind of thinking do you tend to have? You may have a couple of different styles.

A few examples:

Always searching - trying to find out the best thing, probing

Cheerleader - tend to be upbeat and encouraging in your thoughts

Something's always wrong - things don't seem to be to your liking

Worrier - very concerned, taking in all the possible options to find what's right

Fighter - there's always some kind of injustice or imbalance

Underdog - you don't feel fully yourself, constantly the one who compromises

Hero - protector, knows best way

A few more: Scientist, Morning radio talk show host, Used car salesmen, Professor, Spiritual teacher

3 DAY

TODAY'S SPREAD from *i see peace*

✻ Art Prompt

Briefly map life-changing experiences (both positive and challenging) on the *Ghosts and Guidance* worksheet.

These powerful experiences in your life can help give insight and context for some of the beliefs you may uncover through your play here.

❋ Extra Peace Treat: GHOSTS & GUIDANCE

DAY 3

pg. 15

DAY 4

> i was surprised when i first felt peace.
>
> surprised,
>
> because i had never felt anything like it.

TODAY'S SPREAD from *i see peace*

❋ Daily Thought

Using peace as our learning ground to see through illusions, we can begin to see through other illusions we may have. Our experience in society often leads us to create rules or requirements for living, for example *"once this happens, then I can feel peace."* Because of its physical, external focus, the Western world of thought is built on what is provable, linear and rational. What falls outside of these parameters, things like intuition, creativity and imagination are often repressed, denied or judged...this automatically creates a low threshold of possibility for something as core to our being as peace. We've been convinced that we're being good or responsible if we are worrying or striving first and that if we're good enough long enough, we may experience peace at some later point. Being weighed down with guilt, obligation or regret replaces the possibility of inner peace in every moment.

❋ Affirmation

Peace is every moment. For this moment I let go of my thoughts of worry and responsibility and I simply listen to myself say, peace is every moment. I don't have to believe it. I can just listen to myself say it. This is my moment. This is my peace. Peace is every moment.

a quick BITe of peace

For 1 minute...
Imagine all the cars on the nearest highway or freeway near you running strong and smooth with plenty of room on every side.
Fill each vehicle with love.

❋ Guerilla Peace

Day 4

TODAY'S DATE: _____

✳ Journal Prompt
In my heart of hearts, the one thing I really want to create this year is…

_____
_____
_____
_____
_____
_____
_____
_____
_____
_____
_____
_____
_____
_____
_____
_____
_____
_____
_____
_____
_____
_____
_____

✳ Thought Prompt
Notice the speed of your thoughts. Do you ponder things greatly or do you just have an automatic knowing? Do you tend to act and then realize what you've done or said later? Continue to notice everything about your thoughts.

> i was surprised when i first felt peace.
>
> surprised,
>
> because i had never felt anything like it.

TODAY'S SPREAD from *i see peace*

✻ Art Prompt

Draw. Anything. Begin.

Sometimes it can feel daunting to face the empty page and know how to start drawing. If this is ever the case, notice where your attention is drawn to on the page and drop your pen or pencil or crayon down there. Without thinking too much, allow your hand to be the guide. Don't be afraid to start with a scribble or a round and round motion to see where your hand and the line take you. Your round shapes may evolve into a form or a path or they may just feel fun to do.

If you don't find an image that you want to draw, stick with what feels good to draw. Circles? Squares? Long fine lines close together with red and black circles layered over them? Color, shape, pattern, texture, line are all expressive. Don't feel that you must stick to narrative imagery: *drawings that illustrate your experience*; or representational imagery: *drawings that look the way they are in real life*. Be open to distortion, abstraction and symbolism. The more you allow your hand to freely express the stronger your work will be. Another starting point is to notice if you have some figure or pattern that you have scribbled into margins and notepads for as long as you can remember. Fill your hand with peace and let the creativity flow.

DAY 4

TODAY'S DATE: _____

DAY 5

apparently i had never known what peace was or what it felt like.

peace had been more of a concept.

TODAY'S SPREAD from *i see peace*

❋ Daily Thought

Again, what is peace? After sifting through illusion and other limitations to your experience, you may have a better understanding of peace and just how close or far it is for you. You may recognize that inner peace is not dependent on anything outside of you. It is a sense that rises from the core of your being. It already belongs to you. It is a timeless, unshakable feeling of rightness that radiates out. Consult your heart of hearts, have you ever felt inner peace? Again, acknowledging that you haven't had this feeling, begins to change things.

❋ Affirmation

Today I feel peace in my feet. Whether my feet touch the ground or not, my feet are connected to the Earth and I feel peace. I am a natural part of all things and here I belong. I feel peace in my feet.

a quick BiTe of peace

Copy the *i see peace* cards on page 147 or create your own... Cut them out and begin leaving one here, one there, wherever you go. You can even hand them to people as a thank you. Slip them into jars along with your tip near cash registers, inside newspapers. They work nicely on windshields. Anonymous peace.

guerrilla peace

❋ *Guerilla Peace*

Journal Prompt

The areas I want to most bring peace into my life...

Thought Prompt

My peaceful life looks like...

DAY 5

TODAY'S DATE:

DAY 5

TODAY'S SPREAD from *i see peace*

❋ Art Prompt

Building on your experience with yesterday's drawing, do another drawing that shows the beginning of your journey.

Feel the page open up to you as a place to land. This is a place all your own to express, document, explore. Your drawing may even reveal something to you that you didn't know before.

DAY 5

TODAY'S DATE: _____

DAY 6

TODAY'S SPREAD from *i see peace*

❋ Daily Thought

Whether we know peace or not, it can be hard to put into words. The dictionary says that peace is freedom from disturbance, quiet, tranquility, harmony and calm. These are external representations of peace. Inner peace is defined as *"a state of being mentally and spiritually at peace, with enough knowledge and understanding to keep oneself strong in the face of discord or stress. Being 'at peace' is considered by many to be healthy and the opposite of being stressed or anxious."* The trick is that we can get the idea that our inner or personal peace is supposed to be the same as the concept of outer peace. But if peace is every moment, peace can encompass all feelings. Your peace may be loud and rambunctious at times. Peace comes in every flavor possible. Only you know what your peace feels like and only your words or images can fully express that peace. Play with the idea of expanding your concept of what peace means.

❋ Affirmation

Sometimes my experiences do not need words. They grow in my heart and give me a feeling of peace that is mine deep and true.
A peace that cannot be touched.
It exists. It endures.
It is my eternal core.

a quick BITe of peace

Water connects all of us on our planet...
Filling the seas with peace is a powerful way to acknowledge that we are all connected to each other and to our planet. It's also a fabulous gift for the home of the largest heart that beats. Whale heart! Today and for as long as you can, send peace into our seas. *I am the sea and the sea is me. I sea peace.* Fill the seas with peace.

❋ Guerilla Peace

DAY **6**

TODAY'S DATE:

✻ Journal Prompt

What do you want to create alongside peace?

✻ Thought Prompt

Notice something you have created today. What was the first sign that you were beginning to create? When did you know it was done?

TODAY'S SPREAD
from *i see peace*

✽ Art Prompt

Create...
- 3 symbols that represent a nonverbal experience you have had,
- 3 symbols that represent energy flowing,
- 3 symbols for common and/or rare feelings you have, and
- 3 symbols of thoughts/beliefs.

DAY 6

TODAY'S DATE: _____

DAY 7

> peace affects everything
>
> there is no end to how deep it can go
>
> peace is infinite.
>
> i have only just begun

TODAY'S SPREAD from *i see peace*

❋ Daily Thought

The more you feel peace, the more peace you can feel. Peace spreads out, grows roots, reaches up. Because peace is a natural aspect of your core self, as you become more aware of peace, you will not be able to find an end to it, because there is no end to you. You may find places where your beliefs do not yet permit you to go, but in all things, in all places, there is peace. The more facile you are at seeing and transforming the limitations in your thinking and your beliefs, the more peace is available to you. Those false boundaries will be seen for what they are, old thinking waiting to become new. As you learn to transform your thoughts and beliefs, you will become truly free.

❋ Affirmation

My deep internal, eternal peace touches everything in my life. Although I cannot always feel it, I can trust that I am surrounded by peace. Peace is in me.

Paying Attention...

In every interaction you have today, notice what peace there is. It may be very basic like how cars do not crash into each other. It may be how the bowls nest within each other on the shelf. It may be sitting on your chair and noticing your peaceful weight. Noticing matters. We affect everything with our mind. The more you notice peace the more peace there is.

guerrilla peace

❋ Guerilla Peace

a quick BITe of peace

DAY 7

TODAY'S DATE:

✻ Journal Prompt

Can you see a connection between what you want to create and peace in your life?

✻ Thought Prompt

Peace is all around us. What "hidden peace" can you see today?

pg. 29

TODAY'S SPREAD from *i see peace*

Art Prompt

Similar to the first art prompt, where you drew a picture of your relationship to peace, draw a picture now that shows your relationship to what you want to create in your life.

DAY 7

TODAY'S DATE: _____

DAY 8

> i didn't know someone like me got to have peace.
> i have been clumsy in life but peace belongs to everyone. everyone can have peace.

TODAY'S SPREAD from *i see peace*

❋ Daily Thought

Many of us have been taught in our families, our communities or through society, knee jerk beliefs in good and bad, right and wrong, punishment and reward. We may even convince ourselves that we do not deserve peace or peace is not available because of this kind of thinking. We may think we've done something wrong and it may be true. For whatever reasons, we may have behaved in less than our most idealistic way at times. We may have shame. We may even have hurt others. Or we may have been in the position of being hurt. Others may have used power over us. We may feel damaged. Or used. In one way or another, we may question our value and doubt our worth on a very deep fundamental level. But now please know, peace comes from your core, it is untouched by your beliefs and experiences. Peace is a constant and eternal part of your inner self. No matter what. No matter what. Your core is peace.

❋ Affirmation

I am deserving of peace because I am peace. In every way throughout my day I attract peace. But no matter what is going on in my life, there is a constant sense of connection with my deep inner core where I am peace.
I am peace.

a quick BIte of peace

In your imagination...

Radiate out a wave of peace in your local vicinity. Include the people that you live near. If you live in the country, include the land and animals. Send out your peace to connect with the peace within all things.

❋ Guerilla Peace

DAY **8**

TODAY'S DATE:

✻ Journal Prompt

What if anything stands between you and your peace and what you want to create?

✻ Thought Prompt

Notice if thoughts of regret, obligation and heavy responsibility enter your daily thoughts.

TODAY'S SPREAD
from *i see peace*

※ Art Prompt

Create a drawing to represent your thinking throughout the day, or in general.

For example, is your thinking huge and expanded, or does it feel small and fixed? Does your thinking feel all over the place or cohesive? Maybe you have a sense of a bigger, intuitive thinking that oversees your life? Often how we think in the big ways in our life, are present in our daily thinking. So you could start there if you like.

DAY 8

TODAY'S DATE: _____

DAY 8: Seeing Your Thoughts

i didn't know someone like me got to have peace.
i have been clumsy in life but peace belongs to everyone. everyone can have peace.

TODAY'S SPREAD from *i see peace*

Listen to yourself, listen to your thoughts and write them down in the **Seeing Your Thoughts** worksheet.

Don't choose the ones that are about keeping track of your day. Choose the thoughts inside those thoughts. The ones that say, *I have too much to do today. I never get any support.* If you can't see those ones, **notice the kinds of thoughts you're having**. Are you constantly thinking about what you have to get done? Are you worrying about people or circumstances? Are you judging yourself or the situation in some way? *I always eat too much. I don't get enough exercise. There's too much to do. He never does things right.* OR, *are you thinking the sky is expansive and beautiful? Things always work out in the best way possible. I love it when that happens. I am beautiful and strong. I am happy working right now. I love you, _____.*

When you notice a thought write it down in one of the squares that best categorizes it. In the center, write in any **thoughts related to peace** in these 4 areas.

Do this until you have a nice sample of your thoughts or you just don't want to do it anymore.

Afterwards take a good look, notice any patterns. *Are there places where your thinking is stronger and more steady and positive than others? Do your thoughts differ widely between areas or do you have a similar way of thinking about everything? What areas seem to be working well and what areas are you wanting change?*

If you look closely you may notice that your thoughts fall into groups. In fact, **a lot of times, we're having the same thought from a million different angles.** Are there any thoughts that epitomize your thinking? For example, *life is hard and then you die*. Or maybe a little less dramatic, *life is a struggle, you just have to do the best you can*. Or even, *life is a river, you just gotta flow*.

Extra Peace Treat: SEEING YOUR THOUGHTS

DAY 8

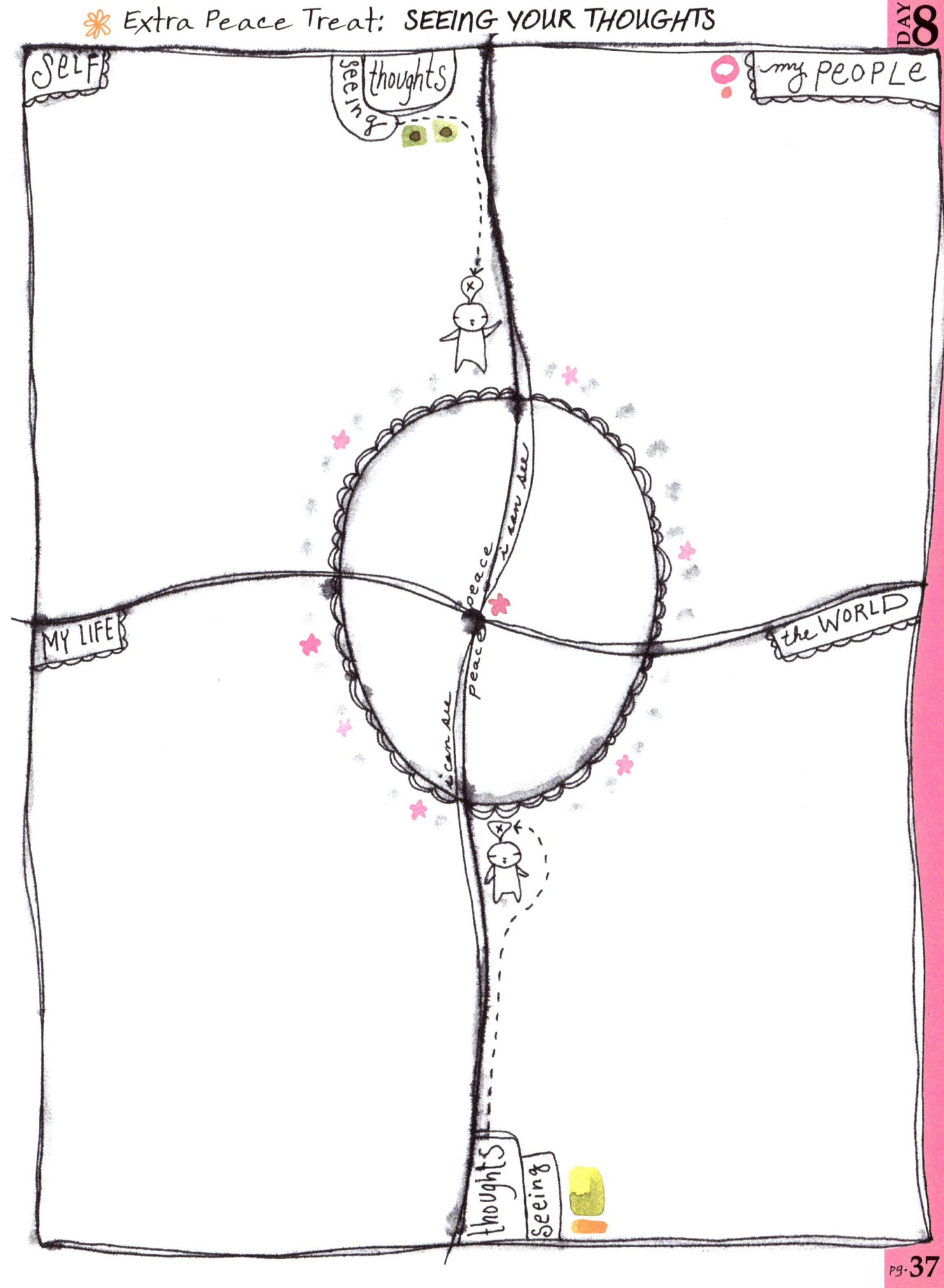

DAY 9

TODAY'S SPREAD
from *i see peace*

(spread shows: "because peace begins within")

❋ Daily Thought

Unlike happiness, peace is unconditional. Peace is not dependent on anything on the outside, because peace comes from the inside. Once you become familiar with your inner landscape and are more and more able to see your beliefs, you will be able to see through the beliefs that do not fully support your deepest self. As you see through the beliefs that do not support you, you will naturally begin to open up to new beliefs that do support you. Most of our beliefs develop unconsciously. Now you can begin to create the beliefs you want--consciously.

❋ Affirmation

It is easy for peace to grow in my life because I am peace.
Creating more and more peace is perfectly natural for me.
I am like a tree of peace, a sea of peace, a sky of peace.

a quick BITE of peace

With someone you are around today...
simply send them peaceful thoughts.
Don't tell them you're doing this, just do it quietly to yourself.

Guerilla Peace

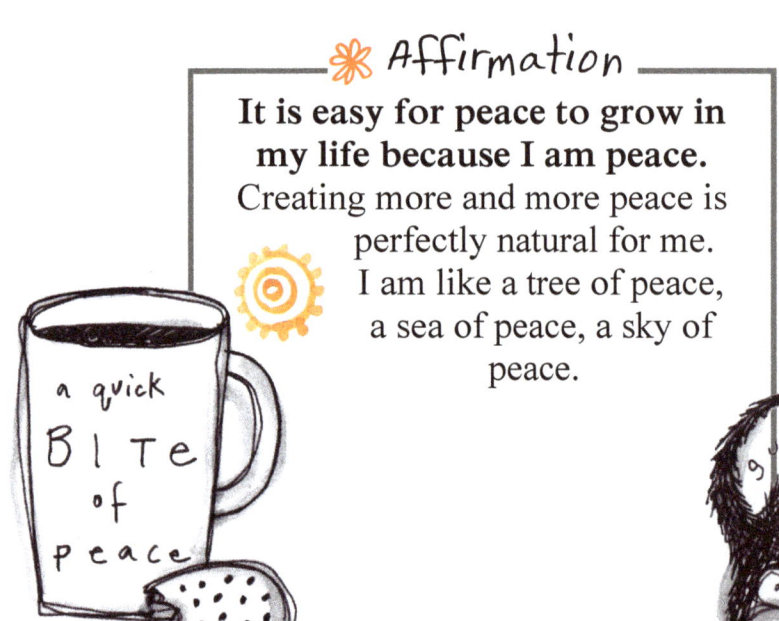

DAY 9

TODAY'S DATE: _____

✻ Journal Prompt

With the *Art Prompt* on the following page, draw your inner terrain and then describe it here. Or if you prefer, describe your inner terrain here first.

✻ Thought Prompt

Bring your awareness inside today whenever you can. Go within and just say, *I'm listening*.

9 DAY

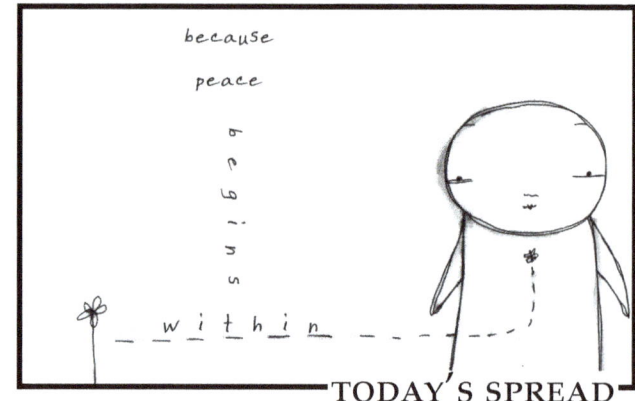

TODAY'S SPREAD from *i see peace*

❋ **Art Prompt**

Draw your within. Your inner terrain. How do you see your inside world?

pg. **40**

DAY 9

TODAY'S DATE:

DAY 9: Seeing & Understanding beliefs

TODAY'S SPREAD from *i see peace*

After you've completed the **Seeing Your Thoughts** worksheet on page 37 (Day 8), Look at your thoughts.

I encourage you to play with the peace thoughts that you wrote in the center area first before moving on to other thoughts. Peace is a perfect place to practice.

You can use the **Seeing and Understanding Beliefs** worksheet on the next page with as many thoughts as you like or you can do it with just the ones that stand out to you intuitively.

Write the thought on the first line, then use your imagination to uncover 3 beliefs you think might have led to this thought.

For example the thought, *"I never have enough time."*
Beliefs that could lead to this thought would vary from person to person, but **3 possible underlying beliefs are:**

1. I'm the only one I can count on.
2. I have to do everything.
3. I can't trust that things will work out.

Keep a playful spirit. You'll know if you hit on beliefs that resonate with you because you've been listening to your inner self. Uncovering beliefs is a powerful tool.

Finally, imagine the effect these beliefs may have on your life.

For example (from the 3 beliefs above) an effect may be, *"I'm always mildly stressed out which affects my health. I have a lot of mistrust in my life. No matter what, I feel there's always more to do, I can never rest."*

✱✱✱Make sure you don't just notice challenging thoughts.

Savorsavorsavor the tasty thoughts too!

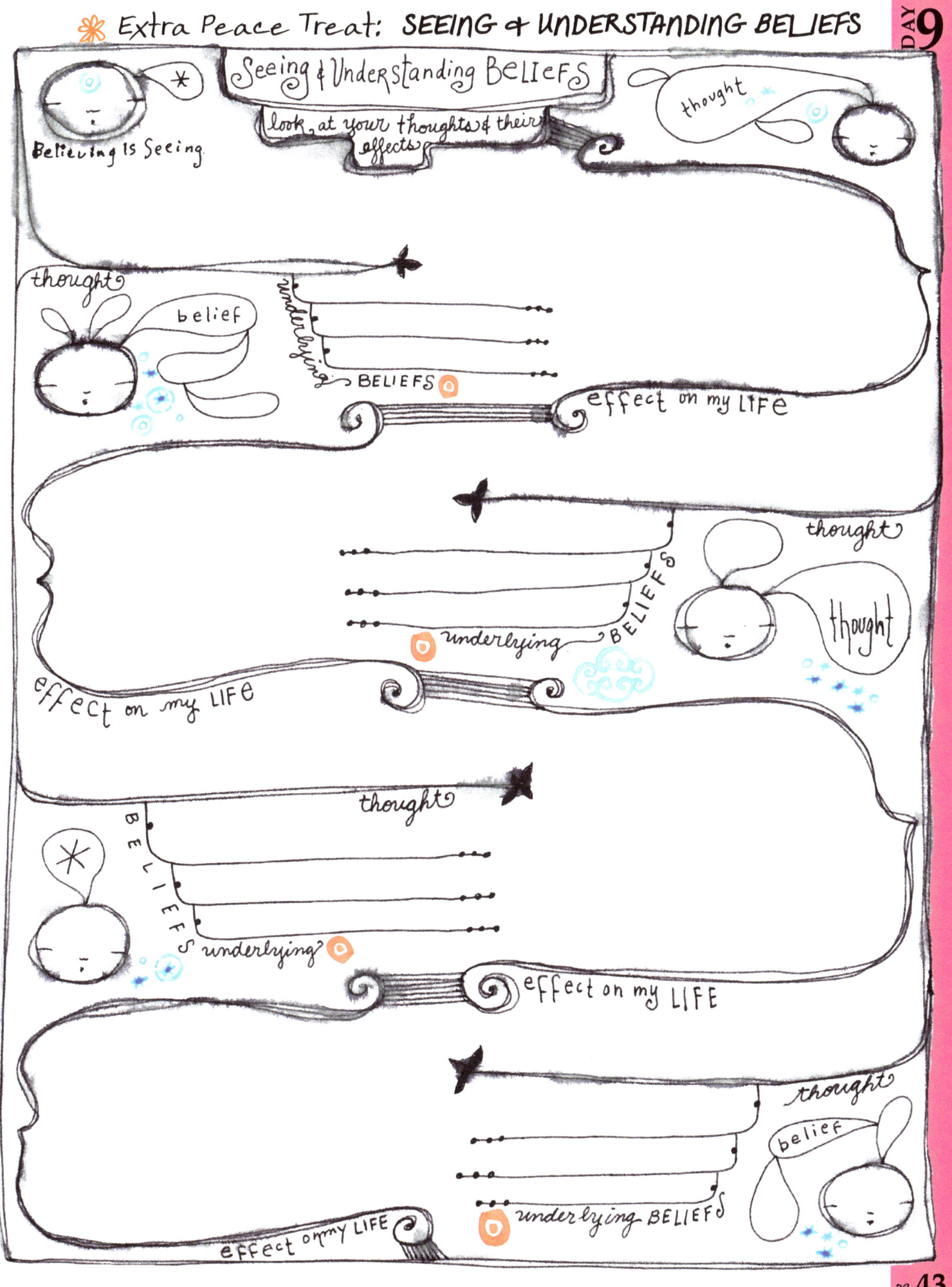

DAY 10

> how?
> when i listen to myself
> (all) of my thoughts, my feelings and intuitions,
> i learn to trust myself
> and peace begins.

TODAY'S SPREAD from *i see peace*

❋ Daily Thought

Becoming familiar with your inner terrain means paying attention to your thoughts, feelings and intuitions. Many of us barely notice what we're thinking or feeling we're so focused on what we need to do in the physical world. Paying attention to our inner selves can feel foolish and indulgent. Many of us are also so well indoctrinated into caretaking others that it can feel wrong to attend to yourself first. With this in mind, getting to know your inner self is like any relationship. It takes time to develop. You need to listen and try to understand. Be kind and curious. This builds trust and allows you to go deeper through experience. We have become so disconnected from our inner selves, we must allow a relationship to develop slowly and surely. Almost like a good friend, listen to your thoughts. Listen to what's underneath the thoughts in your head. Listen to your heart and your hunches. This will create more flow in your life.

❋ Affirmation

It is wise to listen to my heart and my hunches. I am learning to listen to my inner self. This connects me to the peace at my core and supports greater creative flow within and between all areas of my life.

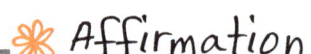
a quick BITe of peace

Choose someone in particular who you know is having a hard time.... It may be someone you know personally or a public figure. Shower them with thoughts of peace. Envision them as deeply at peace in their lives.

❋ Guerilla Peace

DAY 10

TODAY'S DATE: _____

❋ Journal Prompt

When I listen to myself I hear...

❋ Thought Prompt

What is something you think about, but don't even admit to yourself that you think about it?

pg. 45

DAY 10

TODAY'S SPREAD
from *i see peace*

❋ **Art Prompt**

Create a drawing of your relationship with your thoughts, feelings and intuitions.

DAY 10

TODAY'S DATE: _____

DAY **10**

Seeing Your Feelings

> how?
> when i listen to myself
> (all)
> of my thoughts, my feelings and intuitions,
> i learn to trust myself
> and peace begins.
>
> TODAY'S SPREAD from *i see peace*

Extra Strength Peace; SEEING & IDENTIFYING FEELINGS

In Western culture feelings are often unfamiliar.
Many of us lack a full understanding of the feeling aspect of ourselves. It can be hard enough to talk about peace, let alone joy, sadness, grief, pleasure, fear, anger. Consequently, most of us do not understand how to effectively 'have feelings.'

Feelings are meant to *move* through us, emotion. But many of us mix together our body sensations with our thoughts with our feelings creating a system that holds onto feelings, not allowing them to be fully expressed and released.

While, this is a study unto itself, each of us has an intuitive sense of how to realign ourselves. **There are three basic elements to the process that interact with each other in an ever changing balance.**

- Working with our thoughts and the underlying beliefs
- Learning to let feelings move (physically and emotionally)
- Using our imagination/creativity

Letting emotions move through us can feel challenging at first when we find ourselves faced with feelings that are not the ones we want to have. Most of us don't relish the idea of feeling fear or sorrow. But there are ways to have feelings move through us with greater simplicity. If we can remove judgment about which feelings are good or bad, right or wrong, we can just *feel* them.

The best way to just feel is to take the story off the emotion and let the feeling move through you.

So often we'll fixate on part of the story, the core of the pain, with a mantra in our thoughts that will keep us rolling over and over on that one emotion--without any real movement, effectively keeping it in place.

For example, *"Nothing ever works out for me, I'm all alone in this!"* The feeling may rise and peak and come back down, which is excellent to notice, but it will come back again. It may not come back with the same ferocity over time, or it may, but it will always come back, relatively intact with the same thoughts that keep you rolling in the same place.

Something happens when we take the story off of our emotion. It becomes free. Mobile. I'm not saying you will not feel grief in this life if you change your beliefs and pay attention to your body. But **emotion can move through you like a strong river that feels cleansing and leaves you feeling alive and energized**, if you remove the story as much as you can when it's moving through you. The amazing result is a coherence and an inner, organic organization that will build and build.

Because all systems are connected, you will find you have clearer thinking after doing this. **Your thoughts will flow more as your feelings flow more.** It almost goes without saying that your creativity will also flow more.

To begin with, all you have to do <u>right now</u> is notice your feelings. Begin to know your emotional self more. **This is a radical and valuable step.**

DAY 11

> when i can see
> all of me
> without
> j
> u
> d
> g
> m
> e
> n
> t
> ❈
> peace begins.

TODAY'S SPREAD
from *i see peace*

❈ Daily Thought

Like any good friend, listen to yourself with an open mind. Try to understand yourself with a kind heart and remember the map of your life. We often pick up unsupportive beliefs unconsciously, during stressful or traumatic experiences and when we're very young. These are not truths. Only beliefs we picked up to get by. When our beliefs are not visible, they can feel like truths and we can easily judge ourselves as good or bad, right or wrong. There is no need for judgment, only awareness and patience. Opening up to see your beliefs for what they are, changes EVERYTHING. This is how you create lasting change, by working with your beliefs first and foremost.

❈ Affirmation

**Without judgment
I see all of me,
I listen to all of me,
I accept all of me.**

a quick BITe of peace

Choose a particular and/or challenging experience or situation....
and think 3 peaceful thoughts in relation to it.

Guerilla Peace

pg. 50

DAY 11

TODAY'S DATE: _____

❋ Journal Prompt

If you judge yourself, how...

❋ Thought Prompt

Be aware of judgmental thoughts, toward yourself, the people in your life, circumstances, life, the world, people.

DAY **11**

TODAY'S SPREAD from *i see peace*

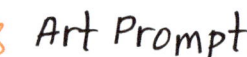 **Art Prompt**

Draw your experience of judgment in your life.

pg.**52**

DAY 11

TODAY'S DATE:

DAY 11
Paying Attention to the Body as a First Step

TODAY'S SPREAD from *i see peace*

Many of our beliefs are frozen in place by repressed feelings. This means that as we begin looking at beliefs long held rigid and firm, we may feel like we're *"coming apart."* It could be disorienting. This is actually a good sign, especially if you know how to support yourself to allow feelings to move through.

Repressed feelings when first approached could feel overwhelming, as if they might obliterate us. We may feel like *"I can't do this."* Or like the world doesn't make sense. You just want to go back to a predictable feeling that everything's familiar and step away from the unknown.

In cases like this, **one of the most important things you can pay attention to is your body.** *Do this first and foremost.* Don't try to calm your thoughts or stop having emotions. You don't even have to slow down to do this. Begin as soon as you can. Just notice everything. Notice if your thoughts are racing. Notice if your chest is pounding, your hands feel cold and clammy or you feel tight in the stomach or chest.

While the Western style of thought is physically focused, it is not focused on the physical experience of being in your body. The focus is directed to the external world and the body is more or less dissociated from except for how it looks on the outside. So for some people this may take practice, especially if you tend to be very mental.

Good ways to begin using the power of your body's presence is to feel your weight. If you're standing notice your feet on the ground. If you're sitting feel your bottom on the chair. If you're lying down feel the whole of your back. If you do not have feeling in these areas, be aware of the weight of your head or hands. Notice the temperature of different parts of your body. *Are there any sensations, tingly, thick, heavy, butterflies in different parts of your body?*

Do a brief inventory, checking in with your feet and legs, full torso, arms and hands, shoulders and neck, face and head. *What is the feeling in each of these areas?* Over time you may notice that energy moves through your body in relatively predictable ways. **But noticing the energy and how it moves will change it.** Pay attention to that too. Notice when things change.

pg. 54

DAY 11

If we attend to the body first, thoughts and feelings will have a more stable container. Since all of the systems are connected, having a stable physical container will help stabilize thoughts and feelings. As these stabilize they will in turn strengthen the body.

So even though we're working with thoughts and feelings, attending to the body first matters most when the going gets rough.

Make sure of course that you're warm and safe, fed and watered. Trust that when big energy in the form of emotions *moves* through, you will become more and more stable. **Feelings are meant to be mobile.** Creating an open channel for them to flow through is our goal. It's not that you won't have hard feelings sometimes. Hard things happen. There are feelings. But they won't get stuck inside of you. They will move through you, **leaving you free.**

How do you know a feeling is moving?

When you pay attention to your body, **you will notice the sensations change.** You may feel warm in different areas. You may even feel tingly, almost like you can *feel* the blocked energy loosening up, moving around and moving out to bigger parts of your body until you can't feel the tingling anymore.

Not only will your body sensations change, but as your body relaxes down again, notice your emotions and your thoughts. It may seem subtle at first, but **over time you will find your thoughts more organized and your emotions more simple, fluid and stable.** When you make a long term practice of this, it becomes your natural default and you become an open channel for feelings to move through you no matter what happens. *In this, there is peace.*

Extra Strength Peace: PAYING ATTENTION TO THE BODY

DAY 12

> when i relax into life and go with the natural and creative flow of my being this for me is peace.

TODAY'S SPREAD from *i see peace*

❋ Daily Thought

There is a natural way that each of us is designed to be. A unique, creative expression of our full self living our full life. The more in line our beliefs come with our inner self, the greater our peace and the more we live this natural way. This lets you access your immense creative flow while supporting everything and everyone else on their path to becoming their full selves.

❋ Affirmation

I belong here in perfect order, I am a natural, creative being of the world.

Choose your favorite way to spread peace in the world today....
You are a peacemaker!

a quick BITE of peace

guerrilla peace

❋ Guerilla Peace

DAY 12

TODAY'S DATE:

✳ **Journal Prompt**

With the *Art Prompt* on the following page, create a portrait of yourself of the true, natural you in flow and then describe it here. Or if you prefer, create a portrait in words first and then draw.

✳ **Thought Prompt**

There are probably moments in each day, where you drop into your own distinct natural way. Notice when this happens. If it doesn't happen, court the feeling and see if you can invoke it.

DAY 12

TODAY'S SPREAD from *i see peace*

❋ **Art Prompt**

Create a portrait of the true, natural you in flow.

DAY 12

TODAY'S DATE: _____

DAY 13

TODAY'S SPREAD from *i see peace*

❋ Daily Thought

When we stand in peace, we will notice others in our life and in the world that also stand in peace. Since we are all peace at our core, we can begin to feel the similarities between all of us and sense our underlying oneness. This allows us to open up to more good feelings not only within ourselves but through our connection with others. Our core peace begins within. When we let it move out, when we are whole and solid in ourselves, when we see peace, we serve as a blueprint and a magnet that naturally draws us into relationship with people who support our truest, deepest self.

Create a drawing or use a copy of the handout on page 148 to.... represent someone in your life who you would like to fill with peace. This is a piece of art akin to a "magic object," a similarity might be a Haitian Voodoo doll. This is like a *Peace Prayer* drawing. Using art or word fill or surround or somehow infuse this person with peace. Allow yourself to drop deeply into the process in whatever way feels right for you. Feel your inner core of peace, imagining their inner core of peace. Keep this a private matter. An inner gift. Unless of course part of what is magic, is for you to share it.

❋ Affirmation

In peace I stand, in peace I am, wholly myself and open to others. As I commit more and more to knowing my inner self and allowing my full truth to flow through my being and my life, I naturally draw people and relationships that support me into my life.

a quick BITe of peace

Guerilla Peace

DAY 13

TODAY'S DATE:

❉ Journal Prompt

What do you desire most in the different relationships in your life?

❉ Thought Prompt

Go back and look at the **Seeing Your Thoughts** worksheet (Day 8/pg. 37) and review the thoughts you wrote down in the MY PEOPLE area. You don't need to do more than notice, pay attention to what you've written.

DAY 13

TODAY'S SPREAD from *i see peace*

✸ **Art Prompt**

Create a drawing that represents how you feel in the relationships you currently have.

DAY 13

TODAY'S DATE:

DAY 14

TODAY'S SPREAD from *i see peace*

✽ Daily Thought

When we begin to see how unique and valuable our own inner peace is, what a big difference it makes in our own lives, we can then understand more and more how true this must be for everyone on the planet. We are all one yet each of us, individually, is a valuable and necessary expression. We need everyone's unique peace. Once we grasp the perfect uniqueness of our own peace, we can also appreciate that everyone's peace is different and simply want others to feel their own inner peace, however that manifests.

✽ Affirmation

I open to the ever unfolding fullness of my own peace and I desire this for everything and everyone. Peace in the earth, peace in the sea, peace in the skies and peace in me. Peace for the creatures, and peace for the trees and everything that grows and flows and shows itself.
I am peace and so peace I see.

In one of your greetings or departures....
wish someone peace along with your usual words.

✽ Guerilla Peace

DAY 14

TODAY'S DATE: _____

❋ Journal Prompt

The people who bring me the greatest peace in my life...*(what it feels like, what kind of experiences, explain the peace you feel with them)*

❋ Thought Prompt

Can you hold the perspective that everyone is completely different and all *one* at the same time?

DAY 14

TODAY'S SPREAD from *i see peace*

❋ Art Prompt

Casting more peace with art and intention. Create a tree of peace. See yourself as a seed and trunk and as you branch out, allow each branch to be someone in your life with whom you experience peace.

You can create branches off of these people if they have brought other people into your life with whom you experience peace.
You can be as imaginative with your imagery as you like. Or you could use something as simple as a family tree model. This tree has an infinite growth potential. Feel that potential at each level. Because we are all peace at our core, this tree already exists in a sense. We are all connected. One eternal tree. We just have to realize it.

DAY 14

TODAY'S DATE: _____

DAY 15

TODAY'S SPREAD from *i see peace*

❋ Daily Thought

Very few have experienced a full inner peace on earth at this time. It is new territory and we can only imagine from our very inexperienced perspective, what kind of thoughts become possible when we are truly surrounded by a world of people at peace. What would be important and necessary in the world? What would fall away? What kind of relationships? What kind of society? We will begin to understand these possibilities more and more because as we have greater peace, we will be drawn to situations and people of greater peace. And together we will begin thinking those thoughts that were not available to us before. And together we will create something new that was not possible before.

❋ Affirmation

I sense the deep inner peace within every person on earth and our connection. I open up to new thoughts and ways of being in relationship that supports the deep inner peace within each of us. I see peace in me.
I see peace in my life.
I see peace in my country.
I see peace in the world.

Spread some peace on a social network....
It could be something you share from your heart or a fabulous banner of some kind or a perfect quote or of course, a piece of your art.

❋ Guerilla Peace

DAY 15

TODAY'S DATE: _____

❋ Journal Prompt
The most important thing I can imagine transforming if everyone felt their inner peace...

❋ Thought Prompt
Entertain the possibility of world peace. Absolute, complete world peace.

DAY 15

TODAY'S SPREAD from *i see peace*

✻ Art Prompt

Create a mandala-like drawing expressing your vision/feeling of world peace.

DAY 15

TODAY'S DATE:

DAY 16

TODAY'S SPREAD from *i see peace*

✻ Daily Thought

As we begin to appreciate and understand on deeper and more personal levels how important and how unique everyone's peace is, we come to see that there are infinite paths to peace. There is no one right path, no one right way. And this is reflected in our relationships. Relationships adjust and evolve as we do, especially as we commit to peace and listening to our inner self. It can be disconcerting if we've built our life on outside expectations. People want us to be who we were to them, even if we weren't being true to ourselves. Committing to peace may initially bring adjustment to relationships. Sometimes this adjustment means that we must let go of the old form in order for a new, more supportive form to rise. Trust that as you allow your relationships to transform through peace, you are supported. Peace has your back, as someone put it. Often relationships serve their purpose, last their time and come to completion. Letting go in peace and honoring what you've learned is a powerful step toward peace.

✻ Affirmation

Inner peace is my guide in relationships. As I change and commit to my inner peace, I trust that peace has my back because peace is my core. With this deep inner part of myself, I create relationships that support my whole, true self.

a quick BITe of peace

Peace be with you....
In your imagination fill yourself with peace as you imagine some challenging relationship or separation that you've gone through. Remember that your peace comes from your core.

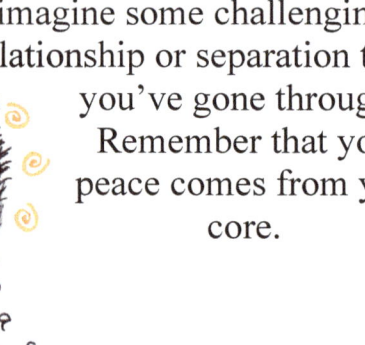

✻ Guerilla Peace

DAY 16

TODAY'S DATE:

✳ Journal Prompt
Write a brief overview of peace in your relationships past and present.

✳ Thought Prompt
Imagine having a life filled with vibrant, alive, peaceful relationships.

DAY 16

TODAY'S SPREAD from *i see peace*

❋ Art Prompt

If you have separated from someone in the past or are in the process of separating from someone in your life now, do a drawing of this person and yourself and show where peace is in relationship to you.

> Be honest. You may wish this person well, but still be holding on to something.

Or perhaps you have a relationship that is challenging. Draw the two of you and your relationship's experience of peace.

DAY 16

TODAY'S DATE: _____

DAY 17

> yes. peace is independent.
>
> we don't have to agree.
> we don't have to be friends.
> we don't have to like each other.

TODAY'S SPREAD from *i see peace*

❋ Daily Thought

There are many things to learn and many paths to peace. Respecting our path and the path of others is very important. We are not supposed to force our connections, we are already *one*. At times it is only by disengaging and separating that peace can grow. The most effective thing we can do is to commit to our own peace and know that only each person can commit to their own peace. The more you understand your deep inner core of peace, the faster and more assured your knowing will be about what relationships and connections are right for you. As you create more peaceful relationships, there is more peace and more to learn about creating peace.

❋ Affirmation

**I commit to my own inner peace.
My peace is independent of anyone else's peace.**

a quick BITe of peace

Share through social media in some way....
this concept, *personal peace through conflict*. It might be a quote or some tidbit of your own personal wisdom or a piece of your art that reflects this.

Guerilla Peace

DAY 17

TODAY'S DATE: _____

✳ Journal Prompt

Maintaining personal peace through conflict, what does this mean? What might it look like? Can you think of any examples?

✳ Thought Prompt

Ponder maintaining personal peace through conflict. You can even just roll over the words. *Peace through conflict. Peace through conflict.* Let it sink in to the nooks and crannies of your thinking.

DAY 17

TODAY'S SPREAD
from *i see peace*

✻ **Art Prompt**

Draw a conflict you have had with someone close or someone casual.

Envision yourself maintaining your peace through the conflict. Draw yourself with this constant peace, even through conflict.

DAY 17

TODAY'S DATE: _____

DAY 18

TODAY'S SPREAD from *i see peace*

there can still be peace between us.

❋ Daily Thought

We are beginning to see how important it is to be our true self. This puts us into direct contact with peace. This is true for everyone. And only our self can do it. No one can do it for us and we can't do it for anyone else. We learn to let other people be themselves on their path as much as we need that from other people. Live and let live essentially. Or, heal and let heal. A valuable thing to understand is that peace does not mean fluffy love all the time. Sometimes peace means different degrees of separation and that's ok. There is a peace in that. So often we think we have to engage and work it all out, when the truth is we may be in very different places. Sometimes there is growth in conflict, but often we are engaged in conflict more for conflict's sake than to resolve anything. Recognizing what is productive engagement and letting go of nonproductive engagement is ok. It's ok to not have relationships with everyone. Live and let live in PEACE. With our family, at work, with our friends, in community, at school, everywhere.

❋ Affirmation

I commit to my peace and I respect that others must commit to theirs. I let go of nonproductive conflict. I let go of thinking I know what's right for others as I let go of thinking anyone outside of me knows what is ultimately right for me. I embrace peace in all its many forms.
I do not judge peace.

a quick BITE of peace

This is a toughy...
Send peace to someone who actively irritates you. This does not mean your irritation goes away. Let it be there too. Both can exist at the same time.

❋ Guerilla Peace

DAY 18

TODAY'S DATE: _____

❋ Journal Prompt

What would your life be like if you could hold onto your peace all the time? How would your body feel, your heart, your mind feel?

❋ Thought Prompt

Keep imagining yourself at peace through the most irritating experience you can conjure.

pg. 81

DAY 18

there can still be peace between us.

TODAY'S SPREAD
from *i see peace*

❋ **Art Prompt**

Create a drawing of what irritates you the most in life, include in it a drawing of yourself in peace no matter what.

Your peace is free and independent!

DAY 18

TODAY'S DATE: _____

DAY 19

TODAY'S SPREAD from *i see peace*

peace is not always smooth it can be gritty.

peace is not always smiling it can be melancholy

peace is like a flower. it is beautiful all the time no matter what feeling is passing through.

❋ Daily Thought

No matter what is passing through you or your life, the essence of your deepest self is peace. It's no surprise that this right here is the essence of deep inner peace. No matter what happens you can have this foundation of knowing. Peace is the essence of your deep inner self and the essence of all things, that creative force that flows through everything. You can have that broad, cosmic perspective that everything is ok. Really. No matter what happens. No matter what feelings pass through you. No matter the loss, the change, the grittiness of the moment. There is a fierce flower that is your soul. It is eternal and this is really who you are. This is the greatest lesson to be learned from being yourself fully from the inside out. As this becomes more of how you identify yourself then the whole nature of your life changes. You will still learn things, but you can know that you are more and so much less than you thought you were.

❋ Affirmation

No matter what is passing through me and my life, the essence of my deepest self is peace. Peace is the fierce flower of my creative soul. I have only to turn my attention to my deep self to access this peace. Because I can sense this truth, I am open to knowing and clarifying the beliefs I have that stand in the way of this. I trust that peace is mine. I will find my way.

a quick BITe of peace

Guerilla Yourself...
Treat yourself to the most peaceful experience you can today. Don't go with your first thought, explore your second and your third thought. No judging. Pure listening. Treat yourself deep.

❋ Guerilla Peace

DAY 19

TODAY'S DATE:

❋ Journal Prompt
Here are 3 ways that I know my core is peace...

❋ Thought Prompt
Ask your inner self to show you your peace during one of the grittier moments of your day.

DAY 19

TODAY'S SPREAD from *i see peace*

❋ Art Prompt

Draw the grittiness in your life alongside the peace within you.

If you don't have grittiness in your immediate life, (fabulous!) allow yourself to expand your vision until you find grittiness. In your family, your community, the country or the world. Holding this vision on any level contributes to welcoming peace into the world. Thank you!!!

DAY 19

TODAY'S DATE: _____

DAY 19: Finding the Belief underneath

TODAY'S SPREAD from *i see peace*

🌼 **tracking a personal experience as an example**

I find my understanding of things is often greatly accelerated when I hear someone's personal account of a similar experience. I was excited to document this rather classic experience of projection and the steps I've learned to see through it.

☼ **THE SITUATION:**

1. **I had been fixating on someone and thinking that something troublesome in my life was really about them.** I knew conceptually that this wasn't true and that this only had to do with me, but I couldn't see through it. It really "seemed" like this person was responsible in some way.

   I was stumped by my perspective as well as frustrated with this "trouble" in my life.

2. **I set up a structure for my experience to support me in listening to my inner self better.** I was committed. I really wanted to get to the point where I could hear the voice underneath and understand what was really going on with me on that deeper belief level from which I created this situation.

What made it trickier is that I knew I could have a line around the block of friends, family and probably even strangers in total agreement with my fixated, blaming thoughts. **I had to stay very strong in the fact that...**

I believed by looking at this deeper level, I could dismantle this troublesome experience in my life by looking at my underlying beliefs.

DAY 19

Here's a breakdown of what I did and what happened:

☼ WHAT I DID:

1. **I paid attention to my body and my felt experience without trying to change anything.** Pure noticing. Just being present with the moment and what was happening inside of my physical body.

    a. I felt heavy in my body. I felt thick and like everything was hard to do, like there was a great weight all over my skin and inside of me. I also sensed a lot of energy stuck in my head because I kept having repetitive thoughts about this person and the situation. I was VERY uncomfortable in every way.

2. **I did not believe my repetitive thoughts.** I just noticed them. I let them be there like they were visitors without trying to make them hurry up or go away. I did not judge them. Just looked at them as neutrally as possible.

    a. I knew there was something going on in part because my thoughts were all the same. No creativity. No flow or movement. All pretty much the same set of thoughts twisting in one place, not going anywhere. And a lot of them!

    b. I could feel myself want to project my feelings onto someone or something outside of me, specifically this person and the situation. I could tell I wanted to obsess on something. Make something work out different, or figure it out or make it ok, just to get back to a happy feeling. Any happy feeling.

3. **I felt the feelings without trying to make them go away.** I did not judge my feelings. Just noticed everything about them.

    a. Although it wasn't totally obvious, I could sense that there was fear.

    b. I did not want to feel fear. I was afraid if I felt it that I might have to make some horrible realization and I was afraid that this realization could take my whole life apart.

4. **I gave it time.** I did not judge how long it would take. I told myself there was plenty of time for this and it was totally worth it.

    a. I had to really relax INTO the discomfort. Give myself over to it almost. Feel it fully and this took a moment because I was so resistant. I had to say supportive things to myself to stick with it. I wanted to turn away, but I knew that wouldn't get me anywhere.

❋ Extra Peace Treat: FINDING THE BELIEF UNDERNEATH

continued on next page →

DAY 19

☼ **WHAT HAPPENED:**

1. My thinking expanded. As it did, I kept reminding myself that this only had to do with me, to keep me on track.

    a. Seemingly out of nowhere, I began having a much broader perspective. I remembered things from my past that were related and began seeing my own overall pattern. I remembered what I had been learning then and although this was a little different, it had so many striking similarities that I could not ignore it. I made a leap that the situations were connected. This intrigued me.

        i. So my thinking not only changed I became curious and interested about these arriving thoughts.

    b. I allowed my thinking to move freely as it became more expanded and mobile. This allowed me to make connections and have deeper insight.

        i. The direction of my thoughts was a clue. I did not think linearly, but in a more mandala shape, becoming aware of the bigger lessons going on in the situations.

        ii. Specifically, this turned out to be a family related belief.

            1. I thought of a past experience.
            2. Remembered what I was learning-or not learning-at the time.
            3. This led me to think of how it related to my larger family experience.
            4. This led me to my experience with my mother.
            5. My mother has been an enormous lesson for me so I could safely assume that I might have something even deeper that was rising to be resolved in relation to the beliefs I picked up from her.

    c. As I freely explored the lesson related to my mother, I began to see how this was playing out in my current situation.

        i. It wasn't and it was the same lesson I was learning 30 years ago! I had replaced the main characters and the situation, but I could see why my thoughts had led me in this direction. The connection not only seemed clear, it felt right.

    d. I understood the core belief that was functioning at the root of my discomfort, which included my attachment to projecting onto someone in particular in my life. It's like it was a small cluster of beliefs with a main belief functioning as the heart of the matter.

    e. My thinking remained open and insightful.

Extra Peace Treat: Finding the Belief Underneath

2. **My body changed.**

   a. I began to feel lighter in my body, as if the weight was slowly lifting. I think this happened before my thinking opened up.

   b. My body continued to feel lighter and lighter. My mind continued to open up more and more until I felt alive and awake!

3. **My feelings moved through.**

   a. A feeling of rightness and even exhilaration steadily replaced my feeling of heaviness and stuck energy in my head. I again felt like my usual happy, peaceful self.

   b. I felt immense gratitude that I knew how to support myself through what seemed immovable.

   c. I felt excited that this shift in perspective would affect my entire life and eventually transform this "troubled" area of my life!

I was so impressed to have had this experience that I audio recorded it right after so I could share it. I think of this as the real "trick."

This process is what I've trained myself to do when I feel stuck, especially when I feel heavy or am having repetitive thinking.

The power is that first part of how to set up supporting yourself to listen to your inner self; that peace within will always find a way to heal through if we give it a chance.

Most of us, myself included, have been taught from a very young age to basically do the opposite of this and it is exactly what keeps us stuck in beliefs that do not support our real inner self, our core of peace.

The other fabulous thing is that the next day I continued to have insights into the mandala of beliefs that were keeping me blind and stuck. The peace just keeps stacking up as I see through what has held me down!

I wish this for everyone. To be freeeee.

DAY 20

sometimes peace is closer than we think.

TODAY'S SPREAD from *i see peace*

❋ Daily Thought

We have been taught to look away, to look outside of ourselves at the physical world for literally everything, even our sense of self, even our own inner peace. Because we have been looking away, peace can feel fleeting. Sometimes easy to see, sometimes we're trying so hard and we just can't see a thing. But peace is there. Slow down. Trust. Listen.

Remember, peace is the natural state of the inner self. *The more you develop a relationship with your inner self, the easier it is to access your peace.* Creating a connection between your inner self and your daily self, or as I like to think of it, the self that drives the car and uses the stove, brings greater peace into your everyday living. Remember *to listen to yourself*, that self under the self, those beliefs under the thoughts, and the feelings that don't move through but stay.

❋ Affirmation

I ask my inner self to guide my daily self toward peace. This is my life and I consciously create the life I desire.
I desire peace because I am peace.

Inner Guerilla...

Receive peace from your inner self and send peace back from your daily self. Create a current of peace flowing between these two points of self. Keep it up for as long as you can stand that much peace.

a quick BITE of peace

guerilla peace

Guerilla Peace

pg. 92

DAY 20

TODAY'S DATE: _____

✳ Journal Prompt
List some of the ways you look outside yourself to find peace.

✳ Thought Prompt
I create this life. I can create anything I want.

20
DAY

TODAY'S SPREAD from *i see peace*

✸ **Art Prompt**

Do a drawing of your daily self connecting to your inner self.

DAY 20

TODAY'S DATE: _____

DAY 21

sometimes we want to believe in peace but it doesn't seem possible.

TODAY'S SPREAD from *i see peace*

❋ Daily Thought

When we look at the state of the world it can seem foolhardy to believe in peace. Everywhere we look the world is being framed and reported as dog-eat-dog. But we've been falsely taught that the world is survival of the fittest. Current research exposes that it is only through grand cooperation that we and all beings, survive. Cooperation is the true nature of nature. It was stressed out humans, separated from their inner self, their core peace, who judged nature as dangerous. We can be part of this new understanding of the world by shifting our perspective on ourselves and nature as a whole. We are not inherently competitive. We are in fact inherently cooperative. Just as we are, at our core, peace. I don't think we can underestimate the effects of this shift in perspective from a competitive survival stance to a cooperative peaceful stance. We are not what we thought and neither is the world.

❋ Affirmation

I live in a safe universe. I open my mind and my heart to the true essence within myself and within all that I see. There is peace, there is cooperation, there is belonging in all directions. The more I shift my perspective in this way, the more I will understand.
I live in a safe universe.

a quick BITE of peace

As you go about your day... visualize the people you come into contact with feeling safe and secure. This is especially powerful in relation to people you feel bothered by in some way. Imagine them feeling a deep sense of belonging and rightness as part of the human family and as a part of the natural world.

guerrilla peace

❋ Guerilla Peace

DAY 21

TODAY'S DATE: _____

✻ Journal Prompt

Explore some of the ways this new perspective will change your thinking...
If I live in a safe, peaceful, cooperative universe, then that means _____ is not what I thought.

✻ Thought Prompt

Each time you notice a fearful thought, remind yourself, *I live in a safe universe.* Be in the moment. Don't over think. Play with your mind.

21
DAY

TODAY'S SPREAD from *i see peace*

✸ **Art Prompt**
Create a drawing of yourself living in a safe universe.

DAY 21

TODAY'S DATE: _____

DAY 22

TODAY'S SPREAD from *i see peace*

but believing that peace is possible is the first step.

❊ Daily Thought

As we begin to see our beliefs and their effect on our inner self, our body and our life, we can begin to entertain the possibility of consciously choosing beliefs for ourselves. We can stop looking outside and start looking inside to our inner self and our core peace for what beliefs we want to hold. Seeing a belief for what it is, feeling the emotions that keep it in place and learning to listen to the inner self are important steps and may, in and of themselves, transform a belief. Often however, there is a leap of faith moment, that moment when we have to put down our old way of thinking and entertain the possibility of a whole new way. While many of us think that we desire peace all the time, in the day to day experience, we may find that we have "limits" on how much peace we are willing to experience. For many of us that leap of faith is simply about believing that we are meant to feel free and peaceful all the time. We are accustomed to living in such a small part of ourselves, at first it may feel like a stretch to become more of who we are. It may even feel uncomfortable. But that is just the old way passing away. Committing to yourself and your living in this way is worth it. Every step counts on the journey to the inner self and you can trust that peace awaits at your homecoming.

❊ Affirmation

I entertain the possibility that I can feel peace all the time.
I respect that it is a journey but that just by committing to this direction I create movement. I trust that peace is my core and that the more I connect with my inner self, the more I know peace. Again, I entertain the possibility that I can feel peace all the time.

a quick BITe of peace

More Inner Guerilla...

Imagine your self within, imagine an inner space, feel the edges of yourself. Now breathe in and expand out beyond this space just a little further. Practice expanding as many times as you like. Know that this guerilla act is not for you alone; you serve as a blueprint for all of us to expand further. Thank you.

Guerilla Peace

DAY 22

TODAY'S DATE:

✻ Journal Prompt
Write a commitment to know your inner self.

✻ Thought Prompt
Entertain the concept that, *I am even more than this. What I think I know about myself is only a fraction of who I am.*

22
DAY

TODAY'S SPREAD from *i see peace*

❋ **Art Prompt**

Create a drawing of yourself making a leap of faith!

pg. 102

DAY 22

TODAY'S DATE: _____

DAY 23

when we believe in something it is more likely that we will see it.

believing is seeing.

TODAY'S SPREAD from *i see peace*

❋ Daily Thought

There is peace everywhere. We're living amidst a wild array of peacefulness, a virtual forest of luxuriant peace, freewheeling and prolific. Inside and out.

It takes a lot to blind us to the true, creative power everywhere to be seen and felt. But our entire way of thinking in the Western world has created and locked a state of blindness into place. That's why we go to the most powerful source of creation to transform our lives, we work with our beliefs. By changing our beliefs, we are not courting denial or ignorance about the state of the world. We are bravely opening up to see what is really real, beyond mainstream media, beyond limiting beliefs picked up as a small child, beyond societal expectations, beyond the materially focused, Western thought. With the knowledge that our core is peace, we can change our beliefs. We can change the world.

❋ Affirmation

**I believe. I believe. I believe…
as I change my beliefs,
I change not only myself,
I change the world.
I believe.**

a quick BITe of peace

Get those cards out… yours or the ones on page 147 and put them out in the world. As you place each card, remind yourself - *believing is seeing*. Notice if you've changed since the last time you went card-ing!

guerrilla peace

❋ *Guerilla Peace*

DAY 23

TODAY'S DATE:

❋ Journal Prompt

When I believe _____, I find that I can see _____!

❋ Thought Prompt

Choose a new belief you are adopting. Imagine this belief is symbolically something in your environment. For example, perhaps you are trying to be more relaxed, imagine *the breeze* is a powerful belief in relaxation. Every time you feel a breeze or even a draft inside, allow yourself to relax and believe that the whole world is supporting you in transforming your belief.

23
DAY

TODAY'S SPREAD
from *i see peace*

 **Art Prompt**

Do a drawing of believing is seeing.

You can focus on the concept or you can focus on a specific belief that you would like to transform...believe it, see it, draw it out!

DAY 23

TODAY'S DATE: _____

DAY 24

TODAY'S SPREAD from *i see peace*

❋ Daily Thought

There are two places where we can come into direct contact with the truth of the inner self. One lies within, as you have been exploring. The other great within, is nature. And truly, nature is all around us. Dirt, birds, sky, wind, weather. Even in urban environments, nature is everywhere. Paying attention to nature is a powerful way to understand the nature of the inner self. The deep, constant need for growth, flow, cooperation, expansion. Nature also shows us the grittiness, the eternal, even the melancholy along with exuberance, wild and free. It is the face of peace.

When we look within, we are facing nature because we are a part of nature. We are looking deep into the heart of nature by looking deep into our own heart. When we look out at nature, we are also meeting our self because we are a part of nature. Looking out at nature is just as much a way of looking deep into our own heart.

❋ Affirmation

**In the sky I see peace.
On the earth I see peace.
Peace is everywhere nature and
I am the heart of nature.
I am peace.** With every step, with every breath I feel my belonging.
I am here. I am here. I am here.

a quick **BITE** *of peace*

Send peace out...
to all of you in the form of the entire natural world, but especially any nature you live with. For example, the plants in and around your home, the sky above your home, the earth below.

❋ Guerilla Peace

DAY 24

TODAY'S DATE: _____

✻ Journal Prompt

The part of nature that speaks to me most is _____. I imagine it's because like me, this part of nature is_____.

✻ Thought Prompt

Every single chance you get, remember that you are not separate from nature. You are the heart of nature. One. Belonging. Safe.

24
DAY

TODAY'S SPREAD
from *i see peace*

✸ **Art Prompt**

Create a drawing showing yourself as the heart of nature.

DAY 24

TODAY'S DATE: _____

DAY 25

TODAY'S SPREAD from *i see peace*

> find out where you see peace.
> go about your day, and here and there, say to yourself... i see peace.

❋ Daily Thought

The more you practice, the more you play; the more you open yourself up to seek, the more you will find! You will come into greater contact with and awareness of your inner self, and your peace will naturally increase. As you get to know yourself more in this way, you will find that the journey is yours. *i see peace* will become your words because they belong to all of us. Or they will transform into new words. You will teach us your wisdom of peace in the way only you can. We need you here with us. We need your peace. As you need ours. Your peace is my peace. My peace is yours. Changing your beliefs to value your inner self and recognize the peace that is at your core can become your way of life. Everything within and without you can change from this place. I believe.

❋ Affirmation

I value my inner self and know that my core is peace. Everything is possible, as I transform my beliefs, I transform my life. These simple truths I hold dear and do not forget. I allow this wisdom to grow in me, increase with each day, become the breath I breathe.

a quick BITe of peace

Engage someone in a conversation... about what their biggest dream in life is. Be curious and supportive.

❋ Guerilla Peace

pg. 112

DAY 25

TODAY'S DATE:

❋ Journal Prompt
What I have discovered and value most about my inner self...

❋ Thought Prompt
Throughout the day imagine what you would change in your life. Look about with a big imagination and plot what to transform.

DAY 25

TODAY'S SPREAD from *i see peace*

✳ **Art Prompt**

Create a drawing to remind you of today's affirmation.

DAY 25

TODAY'S DATE: _____

DAY 26

and you will·

it may be quite small.

TODAY'S SPREAD from *i see peace*

❋ Daily Thought

You are becoming more and more familiar with your inner self and your deep inner core of peace. You're beginning to see and your thinking is shifting. You are becoming more you as you come into contact with your true self. This is the most powerful and supported position for absolutely everything in your life. It is an especially powerful position for manifesting what you want.

Pay attention to how you've brought peace into your life. Feel how you have opened up to peace and how it feels when you are in the flow. Peace has been teaching you all along how to create other things in your life. Within you lies the power to create anything. This is the source of your true power. It is not out there in the world. It is right here within you. If you want to affect your outer world in a real, substantial way that lasts, you must begin within. You must begin with you.

❋ Affirmation

Every day, I open myself more to the truth of my inner self, the depth of my peace and my amazing power to create.

My self, my body, my life are the artful expression of my inner self. Trusting that peace is my core, I create a safe universe inside and out. I am free to create the life I imagine.
I am free to be safe and powerful.

a quick BITE of peace

Guerilla Home....

Place small notes about what you're creating in little places just for you.
Peace bomb yourself, your home, your car. Love yourself and your courage to create change and be your full, true, peace self!

guerilla peace

❋ Guerilla Peace

DAY 26

TODAY'S DATE: _____

✽ Journal Prompt

List 3 beliefs that you want to change or are changing to stronger, more supportive ones. How would changing these beliefs affect your life. Be specific.

✽ Thought Prompt

Begin imagining your life as you wish to create it. Begin with the inside. For example, if you're creating more peace in your life, imagine what peace might feel like even when you can't feel it.

26
DAY

TODAY'S SPREAD from *i see peace*

❋ **Art Prompt**
Create drawings about what you want to create in relation to your self, your body and your life. Art prayers.

pg. 118

DAY 26

TODAY'S DATE: _____

DAY 27

TODAY'S SPREAD from i see peace

❋ Daily Thought

There is no limit to what you can create in your life. Through peace you will begin to learn that anything is possible. There is an infinity, an eternity within you. Allow the wisdom of your peace to continue to teach you about how to create everything. Peace is the essence of your deep inner core and this part of you desires more and deeper peace, more you, your deep essence aligning with your daily self, creating your life like the art that it is. You can trust and relax into this part of yourself. This is home. Here. Now. You may not be who you thought you were. The world may not even be what you thought it was. But ironically, you may find that you are exactly who you always thought you were, deep down inside. And the world is as magic now as it was in some childhood moment when you could still see.

❋ Affirmation

I am a limitless, creative being of infinite peace. I trust that my inner self and my daily self are aligned to assist in the perfect creation of the life I desire. The more I let go into these truths, the more effortless and graceful my life unfolds.

a quick Bite of peace

Create a drawing....
of the most important thing you've learned through this journey and leave it somewhere in public. Public could be out in nature, on a city street, down a quiet alley, the grocery store parking lot...listen to your drawing and where it would like to land... and then let go.

guerrilla peace

❋ Guerilla Peace

DAY 27

TODAY'S DATE: _____

Journal Prompt
I am changing right now...

Thought Prompt
Throughout the day, remind yourself in some playful way, **I CREATE MY REALITY, my life is my art!**

27
DAY

TODAY'S SPREAD
from *i see peace*

Art Prompt

Create a drawing of your creative force moving through your body and transforming your life.

DAY 27

TODAY'S DATE: _____

DAY 28

TODAY'S SPREAD
from *i see peace*

❋ Daily Thought

You are your greatest teacher. Establishing a foundation of trust with your inner self provides you with the most important tool you can have. You can trust that. You can trust you and your belonging and your perfection. All you ever need to do is wake up to who you truly are. You will greet peace all around you, as your inner world becomes reflected in your outer world. You are safe. What you create from this place can only make you stronger. It will multiply your sense of peace and creative power because that is your true essence. You fulfill a natural cycle of being.

❋ Affirmation

I am my greatest teacher.
I teach myself in every moment. All I have to do is pay attention to my inner self. I am peace.
Peace is my teacher.
I am my greatest teacher.

Wise Guerilla...

Instead of peace cards, create cards that share one of the most important things you have taught yourself. Share your wisdom.
Randomly leave your cards somewhere, possibly several somewhere's. Remember you can leave them anywhere public. This can be out in nature or some mall's public restrooms. Feel free to let your wisdom out in the world.

Guerilla Peace

Journal Prompt

The most important thing I am teaching myself...

Thought Prompt

Throughout the day ask yourself, *what am I teaching myself?*

DAY 28

TODAY'S DATE:

28
DAY

TODAY'S SPREAD
from *i see peace*

 **Art Prompt**

Create a portrait of yourself as your teacher.
Really see the wise, expanded part of yourself.

DAY 28

TODAY'S DATE: _____

DAY 29

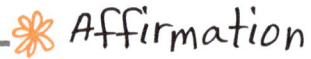

TODAY'S SPREAD from *i see peace*

❋ Daily Thought

Through the art you've been creating in the course and these initial steps of creating peace, you can sense how your own unique creative force moves through you. You can sense what your most authentic and intuitive way of creating art AND peace feels like? This is the same with everything you want to create. Sensing the feel of your individual creative style helps you to access and enhance your creative power as you learn to ride your natural ebb and flow.

Some creations take time with numerous layers of underpainting. Some creations are spontaneous like the swift touch of ink on paper. You will have both. Keep your eyes open to all the different ways you create in your life. Trust that as you have created art on a blank page, you have also created peace in places where before there seemed to be none. These experiences put you in touch with your creative power. This prepares you to consciously create bigger and bigger things in all areas of your life.

❋ Affirmation

The more I sense my individual creative style, the more effortless creating becomes. Peace and creativity are my natural states.

Guerilla Manifestation or throwing your peace around like a pro!

Take a time of your day where you have a lot of different things to get done, maybe you even feel like it's too much. At each step imagine things going even better than you could have initially thought. No matter what, keep saying to yourself, everything is working out better and better.

Journal Prompt

Explore how peace and creativity are connected for you personally.

Thought Prompt: View everything in your life as something you have created in some magical way.

DAY 29

TODAY'S DATE:

29
DAY

TODAY'S SPREAD from *i see peace*

Art Prompt

Create an image that represents peace and creativity together.

pg. 130

DAY 29

TODAY'S DATE:

DAY 29

TODAY'S SPREAD
from *i see peace*

All along you've been working with these different elements. Now you can see an overview of what's involved. Notice that throughout the workbook, the Belief worksheets (*Extra Peace Treat*) are coded in pink and the Emotion worksheets (*Extra Strength Peace*) are coded in green.

Generally, the most effective way to work with this kind of transformation is to go slow and let things take as long as they need to. This allows enough time for feelings to fully move through and new structures and connections to be made. *Not taking on too many beliefs at once is a good way to stay focused and keep things simple.* There is time for all your beliefs to be transformed.

Bringing awareness to your process is very valuable. Take a moment to review your journey. The **4 Elements to Transform Beliefs** diagram on the right can also serve as a quick reminder as to what you've done, what might be good to repeat and/or what you may need to focus on more deeply.

The 4 primary elements to transform beliefs are:

1. Listening to inner self
2. Playing with beliefs
3. Working with emotions
4. Opening up expectation

Feel how these four elements play in your life. Which is your strongest? Where would you like to gain greater ease? Is there an area that you don't fully understand or needs strengthening? Look at the worksheets that you've done so far. Know yourself. Support yourself.

See your creative peace power!

Extra Peace Treat: 4 ELEMENTS TO TRANSFORM BELIEFS

DAY 29
Playing with your beliefs

TODAY'S SPREAD from *i see peace*

Extra Peace Treat: PLAYING WITH YOUR BELIEFS

Take one of the *underlying beliefs* you wrote down on your **Seeing and Understanding Beliefs** worksheet on page 43 (Day 9) and write it in the column for *Beliefs Going Bye Bye* on the **Playing with Your Beliefs** worksheet on the right.

For example, a belief to transform:

"I don't have the education to create a children's book."

To help break up your original belief and explore what new belief you might want, write down its opposite in the next column.

For example, opposite belief:

"I know everything I need to create my children's book."

In the third column write a completely different replacement belief entirely.

For example, different belief:

"I am free to fulfill my dreams!"

Now in the last column write the most loving, unlimited, peace filled belief you can imagine.

For example, most loving unlimited peace-filled belief:

"I am a strong creative person and I effortlessly attract everything I need to create my children's book."

Which of these beliefs do you want to create?

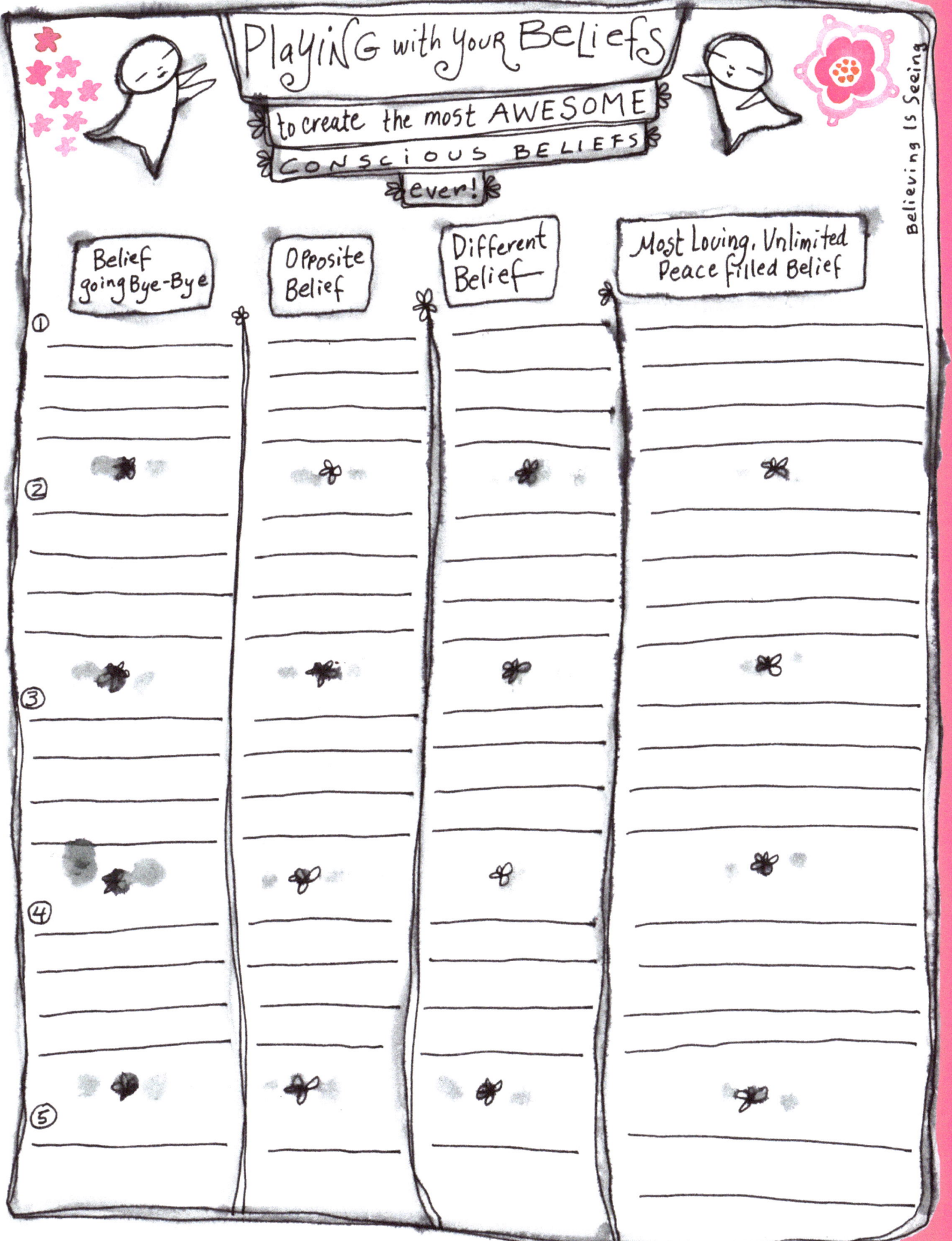

DAY 29 Transforming beliefs

and again.

TODAY'S SPREAD from *i see peace*

Use the following page to begin transforming your beliefs

One-Inner Self/Peace: always check in with your inner self and peace first. Listen to yourself and acknowledge any insight that rises.

Two-Beliefs: choose the belief you want to create from the **Playing with Your Beliefs** worksheet from the previous page and write it down in the space provided.

Three-Emotions: list any emotions that may need to flow in order for your beliefs to transform effectively.

- You can show in your drawing where these emotions are in your body and how they can flow
- Feelings are neither good or bad—let them all flow freely
- Remember peace is always your core
- Go slow, pay attention, relax!

Four-Expectations: this is the last step before the drawing and is very important. Open your heart and your creative flow. **What are you excited about experiencing by creating this new belief?**

Five-Drawing: create! You can draw yourself experiencing your new belief, or show any stuck feelings flowing, or receiving what you are expecting or your inner self and peace supporting you or ALL OF THE ABOVE!

The act of drawing is a powerful way to come into direct contact with your creative force and get that unique feel of your creative style.

Extra Peace Treat: TRANSFORMING BELIEFS

pg. 136

✳︎ Extra Peace Treat: TRANSFORMING BELIEFS

DAY 29

three emotions — List emotions that may need to FLOW to tRANSFORM Belief: (emotion)

- You can show in your drawing where these emotions are in your body + how they can Flow
- Feelings are neither good or bad — let them ALL Flow Freely
- Remember Peace is always Your Core
- Go slow, Pay attention, Relax
- You Rock!

TRANSFORMING·BELIEFS

two Beliefs — State Belief you are creating:

one Inner Self Peace — check in here first INSIGHT

five DRAWING — create!

Believing is Seeing love, make v.

four expectations — Open your Heart, your creative flows about experiencing from this. are you excited what

this is the Last IMPORTANT step

pg. 137

DAY 30

> just say the words
>
> i see peace
>
> and see.
>
> TODAY'S SPREAD
> from i see peace

❋ Daily Thought

Sometimes it is only in hindsight that we can fully receive and appreciate the journey we have been on, the courage we have had, the leaps we have made, the real peace we have created. You are not the same person who began this course. You will never be the same. You are more now and because of that, you will become even MORE, naturally. More creative, more peace filled. The door has been opened. Now you know,

You create your own reality-the more you are you, the better you create—EVERYTHING! It is worth the journey. It is why you're here. It is why we need you.

❋ Affirmation

I am in this body and heart to be my full self. It is in being my full self that I fulfill my purpose here and bring the greatest amount of peace that I can to earth.

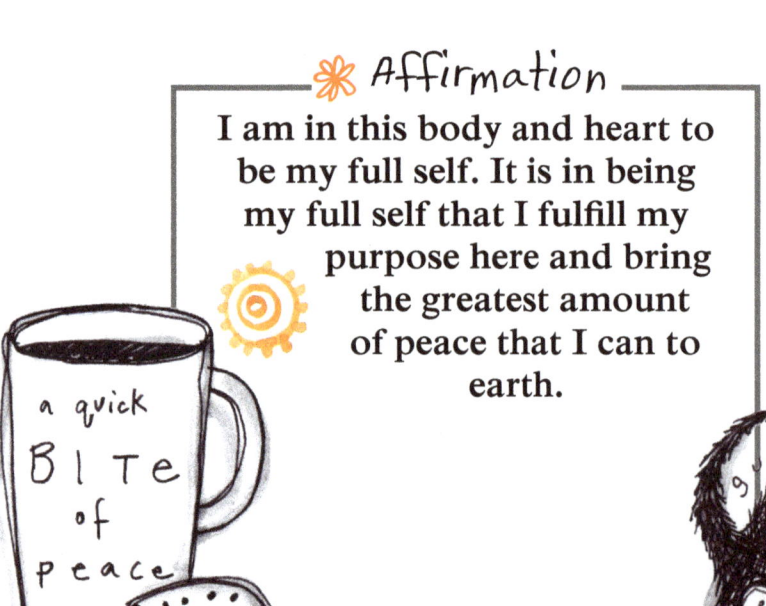

a quick BITe of peace

Neighborly Guerilla....

If you feel abundant, let your peace spill over by calling someone you know who is having a rough go and just listen.
Don't try to solve anything, let them be completely in their experience and hold the thought,
i see peace in you.

Guerilla Peace

DAY 30

TODAY'S DATE: _____

✻ Journal Prompt

When I began this journey, I was _____. Now I see that I am _____.

✻ Thought Prompt

Notice any moments when you feel that you are not being your full self. Notice any moments when you are being your full self.

30
DAY

TODAY'S SPREAD
from *i see peace*

❋ Art Prompt

Create a piece of art of today's affirmation.

Make a copy (or copies!) and put them up in your home.

DAY 30

TODAY'S DATE: _____

DAY 31

TODAY'S SPREAD from i see peace

❋ Daily Thought

Making peace as much of a habit as your morning ritual is just the beginning. When we approach all of life this way, when the inner self and peace are the foundation of life, everything becomes rooted in the very heart of who we are in the biggest, deepest sense. Our body, our relationships, our work, our family, our community and more...Your life becomes one great flow between the inside and the outside, the living and the being become one. This makes you strong as a person and more and more of us strong as a people. You are changing the world. This is the new wave of revolution. This revolution begins within and cannot fail because it is who you are.
Believing is seeing.
i see peace in you.

❋ Affirmation

More and more of my life expresses my full self and my deep peace.

Inner Guerilla....
Fill yourself with peace, over and over and over again, until you feel that you are full.

❋ Guerilla Peace

DAY 31

TODAY'S DATE: _____

✱ Journal Prompt

As I close this time, I consider my next steps. My first thoughts are _____.

Thought Prompt

Say to yourself *i see peace* throughout the day. Make today a special practice as you close this time. Heighten your attention each time you say it.

31
DAY

TODAY'S SPREAD
from *i see peace*

❋ Art Prompt

Create a closure piece for this time.

Look at all of the art you have created through this journey and create one piece to encapsulate your experience.

DAY 31

TODAY'S DATE:

Through this journey you have created a path of peace unique to yourself and set your feet upon it. This path is yours and no other's. You may pause or wander. You may come back again and again, repeating your journey until it becomes embedded in the fabric of your everyday self. You may fly forward with fierce force or feel that you have flown backward, only to find that you have deepened in the place where you stand. Once you begin to understand the nature of peace, you cannot go back. It is a limitless journey. It is yours. You are a peace maker.

Thank you. *i see peace.*
xomaya

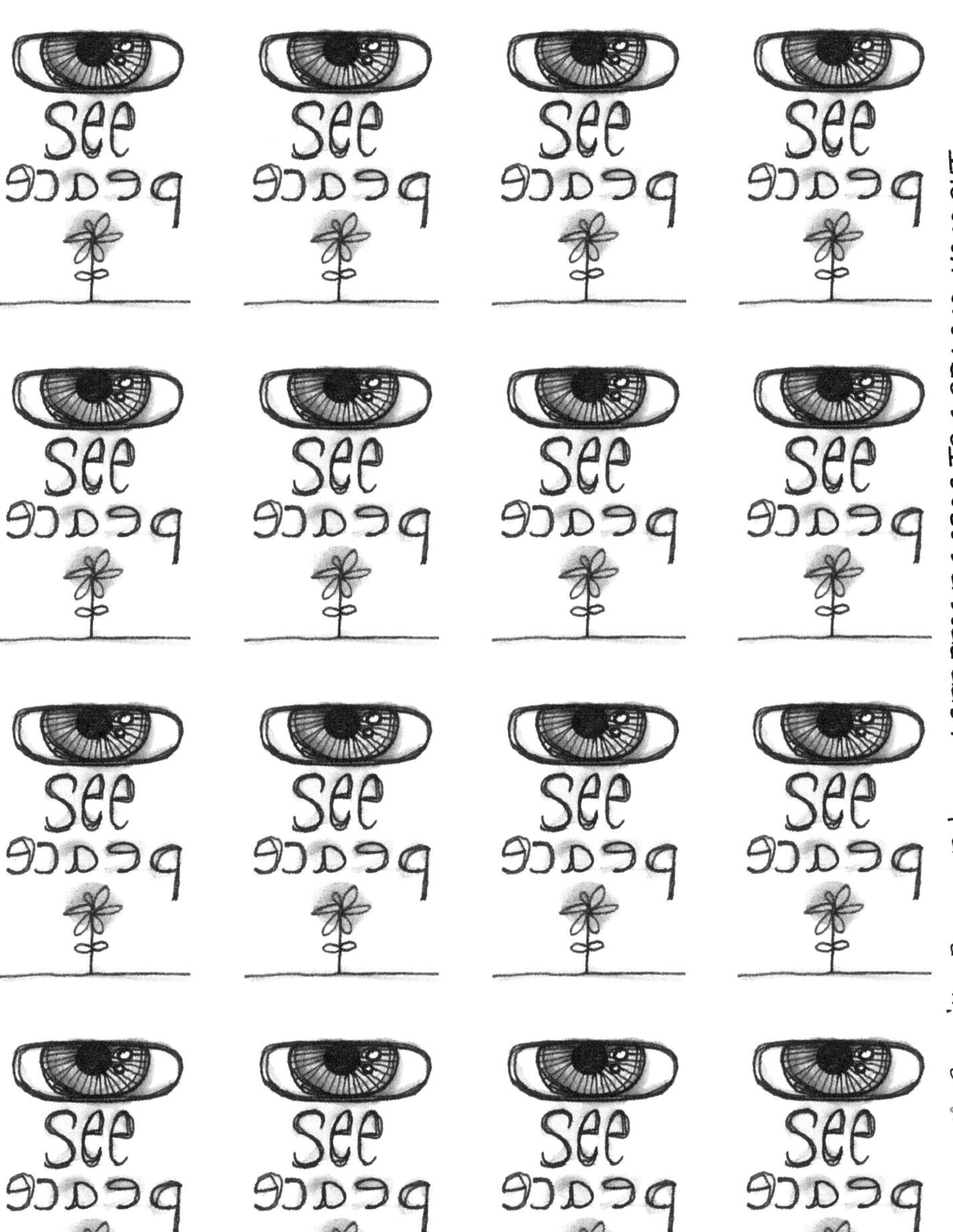

Guerilla Peace Extras: PEACE PRAYER DRAWING

pg. 148

Here's a simple and quick reference matrix showing which days have extra worksheets. It also lists which days have additional audio and video if taking the online course through School of the Free Mind.

Extras in the Classroom (if taking the e-course) Videos & Audio	Believing is Seeing Workbook			Pgs	Day
	Other Worksheets	Belief Worksheets	Emotions Worksheets		
	ART PROMPT: Relationship to Peace			4-7	1
	ART PROMPT: My Fantasy World			8-11	2
		ART PROMPT: Ghosts & Guidance		12-15	3
VIDEO on Using the *I See Peace* book in the course				16-19	4
	GUERILLA ACTION: I See Peace Cards (pg 147)			20-23	5
				24-27	6
				28-31	7
		Seeing Your Thoughts		32-37	8
		Seeing & Understanding Beliefs		38-43	9
			Seeing Your Feelings	44-49	10
VIDEO on Drawing the *I See Peace* character AUDIO Peace for Pain			Paying Attention to the Body as a First Step	50-55	11
				56-59	12
	GUERILLA ACTION: Peace Prayer Drawing (pg 148)			60-63	13
				64-67	14
				68-71	15
				72-75	16
				76-79	17
VIDEO on Drawing Relationships				80-83	18
		Finding the Belief Underneath		84-91	19
				92-95	20
				96-100	21
AUDIO Peace for Doubt & Feeling Stuck				101-104	22
	GUERILLA ACTION: I See Peace Cards (pg 147)			105-108	23
				109-112	24
VIDEO on Illustrating the Affirmations				113-116	25
				117-120	26
				121-124	27
				125-128	28
		4 Elements to Transform Beliefs, Playing with Your Beliefs, Transforming Beliefs		129-137	29
AUDIO Peace for Fear				138-141	30
				142-145	31

Extras; Worksheets & Extras Matrix